Move!

Houghton Mifflin Company Boston

nimals move in different ways.

swing

A **gibbon** swings through jungle trees . . .

. . . or walks on two back legs.

walk

A jacana walks on floating lily pads . . .

. . . then dives in to catch a fish.

dive

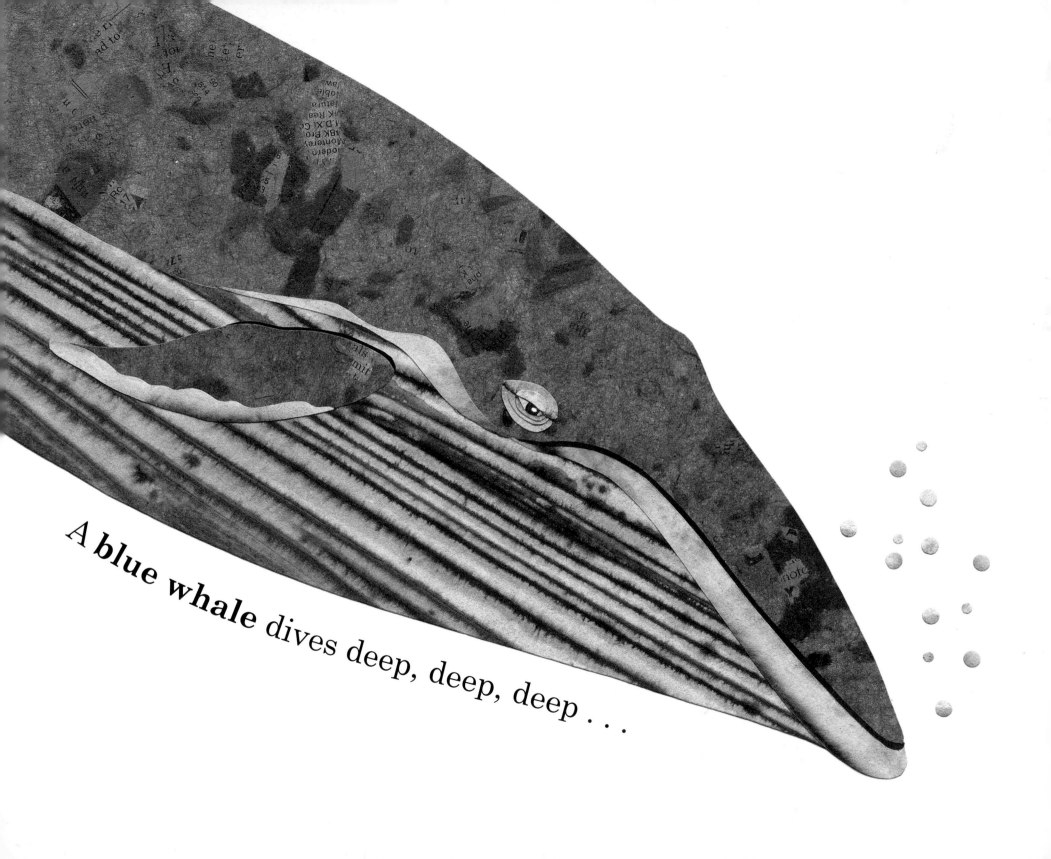

A **blue whale** dives deep, deep, deep . . .

swim

. . . and swims below the ocean waves.

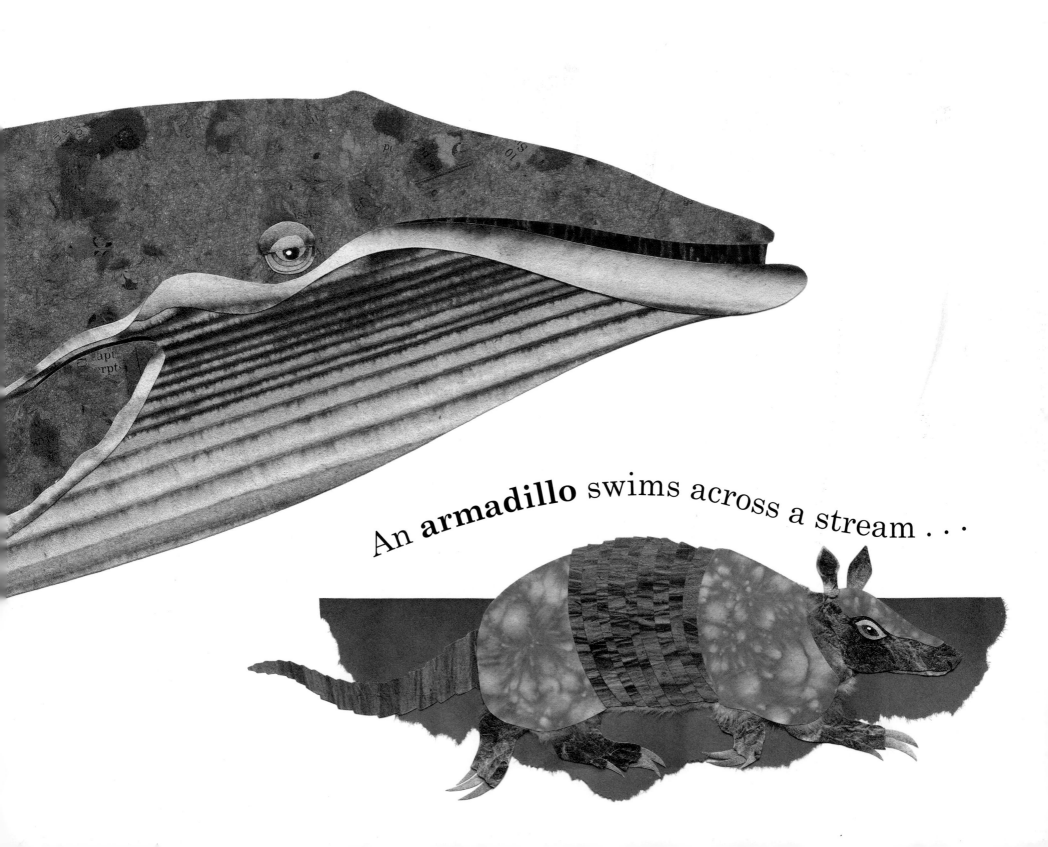

An **armadillo** swims across a stream . . .

. . . and, when startled,

leaps straight up.

leap

A **crocodile** leaps

to snag its meal . . .

. . . after slithering silently into the water.

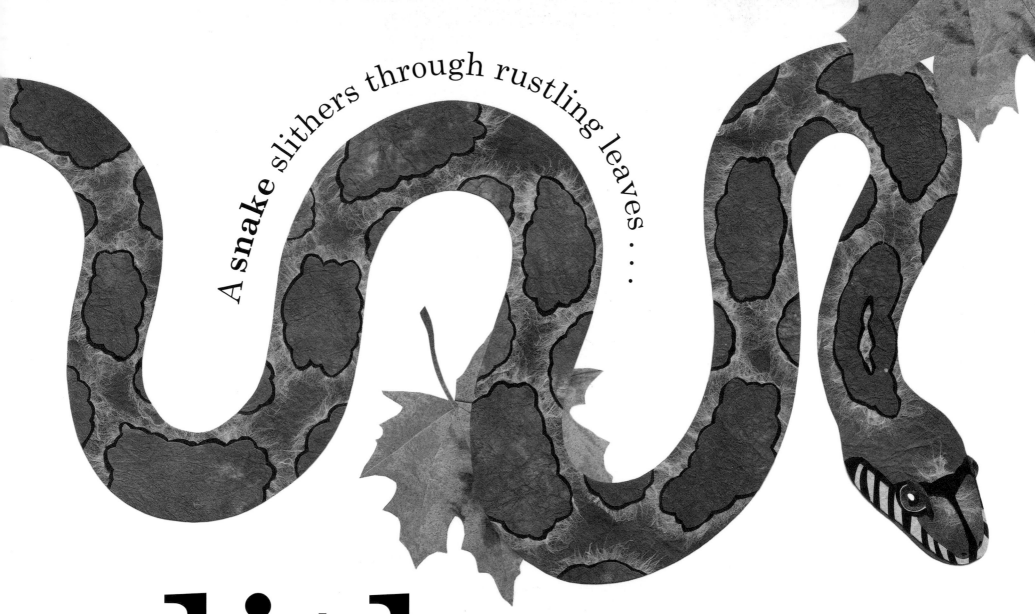

A snake slithers through rustling leaves . . .

slither

. . . and climbs up into a tree.

climb

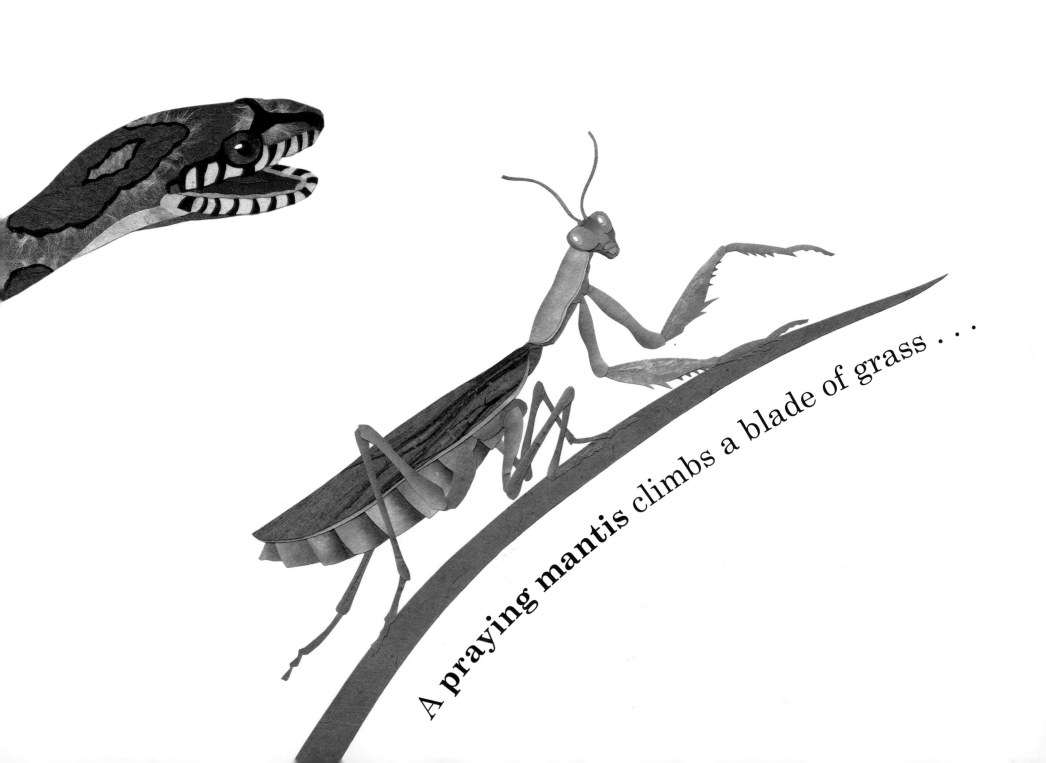

A praying mantis climbs a blade of grass . . .

...then spreads its wings and flies.

fly

A **roadrunner** flies, but not too far . . . .

run

. . . it would rather run to catch its prey.

An **arctic hare** runs across the ground . . .

. . . then dances, tumbling with its mate.

A jumping spider dances to impress . . .

dance

. . . then floats away on a thread of silk.

float

A **polar bear** floats
in dark, icy water . . .

. . . and slides down a snow-covered hill.

A penguin slides — splash! — into the sea . . . .

slide

. . . and waddles with its colony.

waddle

waddle slide float dance run fly climb

Animals move in different ways . . .

. . . how about you?

slither leap swim dive walk swing

Move!

White-cheeked **gibbons** are acrobatic animals that spend their lives in the treetops. Gibbons travel by swinging from branch to branch, sometimes covering more than 30 feet (nine meters) with a single swing. On the ground, they can stand upright and walk on their back legs. Gibbons are found in the jungles of Southeast Asia, where they eat plants, insects, and birds' eggs. A large gibbon weighs about 15 pounds (seven kilograms).

The **African jacana** walks across the surface of the water by stepping on floating lily pads. Its long toes and claws spread its weight out and keep it from sinking. This long-legged bird is also an excellent diver and swimmer. It eats insects and fish and lives in the wetlands of southern Africa. African jacanas are about 12 inches (30 centimeters) long.

Blue whales are the largest animals that have ever lived. They dive deep into the sea and are very fast swimmers. These huge mammals can be more than 100 feet (30 meters) long and weigh as much as 25 African elephants. Blue whales eat only tiny shrimplike animals called krill.

The **nine-banded armadillo** is about the size of a large housecat. It can cross a river by swimming on the surface or by walking across on the bottom. On land, this armored mammal looks slow and awkward, but it can move quickly. When surprised, the armadillo can jump straight up into the air, startling an attacker. Armadillos live in the southern United States and South America. They eat insects and small animals. Strangely, baby armadillos are always born as identical quadruplets.

The **Nile crocodile** is a huge reptile, reaching 20 feet (six meters) in length. The crocodile lies quietly in the water, waiting for an unsuspecting animal to approach. Then, with a stroke of its powerful tail, it leaps forward and grabs its prey with sharp teeth. Crocodiles often bask in the sun at the edge of a lake or river, slithering down the bank to return to the water. They will eat almost any animal they can catch — sometimes even humans. The Nile crocodile lives in rivers and lakes throughout Africa.

The colorful **corn snake** has a flattened belly, which helps it climb trees and walls. Like many other snakes, the corn snake moves over the ground with a slithering motion, forming S-shaped loops with its body. Corn snakes live in the southeastern United States and can

grow up to six feet (183 centimeters) long. They eat rodents and birds and kill their prey by squeezing it to death.

The **praying mantis** holds its front legs folded up in front of its body, as if it is praying. The mantis climbs onto a twig or branch, where it looks just like part of the plant. There it waits, motionless, until an unlucky insect, lizard, mouse, or small bird wanders by. Then it grabs its prey with spine-covered legs and devours it. After its meal, this big insect — which may be more than six inches (15 centimeters) long — can fly to a new hunting spot. Praying mantises live in most warm and tropical parts of the world.

The **roadrunner** is a desert bird that lives in the southwestern United States and Mexico. It can fly for short distances with its stubby wings, but it is better at running than at flying — it can move along the ground faster than most humans can run. The roadrunner eats insects, lizards, snakes, and mice, and is about 22 inches (56 centimeters) long.

The **arctic hare** lives in northern Canada. Its fur is brown in the summer but turns white in the winter, when the ground is covered with snow. When threatened, the arctic hare runs, using its powerful back legs to escape danger. During the spring, males and females perform an elaborate courtship dance, taking turns somersaulting over each other. The arctic hare is up to two feet (61 centimeters) long and feeds on twigs and roots.

The male **jumping spider** performs a dance to impress a female jumping spider, waving its bright red abdomen back and forth. This tiny spider is only about one-fourth of an inch (six millimeters) long. The jumping spider can float through the air by "ballooning" — spinning a silk thread that is caught by the wind. And, of course, it can jump — up to 40 times its body length.

The **polar bear,** the largest of all the bears, may be ten feet (three meters) long. It lives in the Arctic and has a thick layer of fat that keeps it warm and helps it float in the icy water. A strong swimmer and fearsome predator, the polar bear is also a playful animal, rolling in the snow and sliding down snow-covered hills. These bears eat seals, walruses, fish, and caribou.

Penguins live in the Southern Hemisphere, so a penguin would never meet a polar bear in the wild. Penguins waddle slowly on the ground, but when they slide or dive into the water they are swift and graceful swimmers. The largest of these flightless birds are emperor penguins, which can be four feet (122 centimeters) tall. They spend much of their time in the sea, where they feed on fish and shrimp.

For Lily, Lydia, Emma & Jamie

The text of this book is set in Century Schoolbook.
The illustrations are collages of cut and torn paper.

Library of Congress Cataloging-in-Publication Data
Jenkins, Steve, 1952–
  Move! / written by Steve Jenkins and Robin Page ; illustrated by Steve Jenkins.
    p. cm.
  ISBN 0-618-64637-X (hardcover)
  1. Animal locomotion—Juvenile literature. I. Page, Robin, 1957– II. Title.
  QP301.J44 2006   573.7'9—dc22   2005019082

ISBN-13: 978-0618-64637-1

Printed in China
SCP 10 9 8
4500432610